W9-CFQ-075

TURTLES

by John Coborn

yearBOOK

yearBOOKS,INC.
Dr. Herbert R. Axelrod,
Founder & Chairman
Neal Pronek
Chief Editor
William P. Mara
Editor

yearBOOKS are all photo composed, color separated and designed on Scitex equipment in Neptune, N.J. with the following staff:

COMPUTER ART
Michael L. Secord
Supervisor
Sherise Buhagiar
Patti Escabi
Cynthia Fleureton
Sandra Taylor Gale
Pat Marotta
Joanne Muzyka
Robert Onyrscuk
Tom Roberts

Advertising Sales
George Campbell
Chief
Amy Manning
Coordinator

©**yearBOOKS,Inc.**
1 TFH Plaza
Neptune, N.J.07753
Completely manufactured in Neptune, N.J.

Introduction

This yearbook was produced for anyone interested in keeping turtles as pets and perhaps breeding them as well. In the following pages, you will find all the information required.

Turtles truly are the most amazing of creatures, dating back to times even before the dinosaurs. They really have been quite "successful" in the evolutionary sense, having remained pretty much the same for millions of years. It is only at the present time that their greatest challenge has arisen. Heavy proliferation of the human race coupled with urban and agricultural development has destroyed many pristine habitats, and now many turtle species are on the decline.

Those concerned about the survival of turtles as a group (and other forms of wildlife, for that matter) can help out simply by voicing their opinion to the right ears. At the present time, governments do seem to be turning their attention more and more to environmental problems. However, there still remains much to be done, so we cannot afford to be lax in our efforts at any time in the future.

What are YearBOOKs?

Because keeping Turtles as pets is growing at a rapid pace, information on their selection, care and breeding is vitally needed in the marketplace. Books, the usual way information of this sort is transmitted, can be too slow. Sometimes by the time a book is written and published, the material contained therein is a year or two old...and no new material has been added during that time. Only a book in a magazine form can bring breaking stories and current information. A magazine is streamlined in production, so we have adopted certain magazine publishing techniques in the creation of this yearBOOK. Magazines also can be much cheaper than books because they are supported by advertising. To combine these assets into a great publication, we issued this yearBOOK in both magazine and book format at different prices.

CONTENTS

Red-eared Slider, *Trachemys scripta elegans*, "pastel variety." Photo by Isabelle Francais.

Home's Hingeback Tortoise, *Kinixys homeana.* Photo by Isabelle Francais.

African Spurred Tortoise, *Geochelone sulcata.* Photo by Isabelle Francais.

River Cooter, *Pseudemys concinna.* Photo by Isabelle Francais.

Florida Snapping Turtle, *Chelydra serpentina osceola*. Photo by Isabelle Francais.

Western Painted Turtle, *Chrysemys picta belli*. Photo by Isabelle Francais.

Galapagos Giant Tortoise, *Geochelone nigra*. Photo by Isabelle Francais.

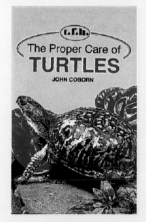

The Proper Care of TURTLES
JOHN COBORN

THE WORLD OF TURTLES

Yesterday and Today

Turtles belong to the order Testudines (also sometimes referred to as Chelonia) in the class Reptilia, which encompasses all the reptiles. At present, there are about 250 species divided into around a dozen families. Members can be found on every continent except Antarctica and occupy a wide range of habitats.

Most people are familiar with what a turtle generally looks like. Turtles are considered rather peculiar, possessing a box-like exoskeleton, also known as the shell, which is fused to the backbone and the ribs and covered with large plates or *scutes*. The top (domed) part of the shell is known as the *carapace*, while the relatively flat underside of the shell (a turtle's "belly") is called the *plastron*. The carapace and plastron are joined along the flanks, with openings at the front and the back to accommodate the head, limbs, and tail.

In many species, the head, tail, and limbs can be withdrawn into the shell. Some turtles have hinges in the plastron so they can withdraw *completely*. In some genera (*Kinosternon*, for example) there is a hinge towards each end of the plastron, whereas in others (*Terrapene*, for example), there is a single hinge in the center of the plastron. One genus of land turtles, *Kinixys*, actually has a hinge towards the back of the carapace which enables it to protect its rear end!

Conversely, many turtles have relatively small shells that leave much of the head, body, and limbs exposed. The anatomy of a turtle usually

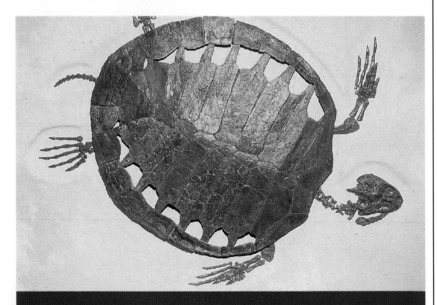

This is a fossilized turtle skeleton found in Utah. The animal is thought to have lived some time during the Jurassic Period. Turtles in general are have been around since the late Triassic, over 200 million years ago. Photo by Alex Kerstitch.

has some relation to its habitat and the way in which it gets its food. Snapping turtles, for example, have small shells, but make up for this lack of protection by being particularly aggressive.

Sea turtles spend most of their lives in the ocean, so they have a very light, streamlined shell. Land turtles, on the other hand, have high, domed shells, making it difficult for predators to get a good grip on them.

As a turtle grows, new layers of epidermal cells form new rings of horny material around the edges of the scutes. Since turtles generally produce one new "growth ring" each year, some enthusiasts estimate the age of particular individuals by counting the number of rings in a scute. This, however, gives only a rough idea of the age because the rings tend to become indistinct in older specimens.

Although turtles are toothless, they do have a tough, sharp-edged beak. The edges of the upper half slightly overlap those of the lower, making it easy for a turtle to shear its food. Some of the more ferocious turtles, such as the aforementioned snapper, have such strong jaws that they are able to cleanly bite off pieces of their prey. Large fish often sport scars as proof of this.

"Soft-shelled" turtles lack the horny plates seen on other turtles. These plates are replaced by a tough leathery skin. Like the snapping turtles, soft-shells can be quite ferocious and can easily deal with most predators.

Testudines form one of the oldest groups of terrestrial animals. They probably arose from the Cotylosaurs, a primitive group of reptiles, during the late Triassic period, some 200 million years ago.

Modern turtles generally are placed into two subfamilies: Cryptodira, the straightnecks, and Pleurodira, the sidenecks. The straightnecks have the ability to retract their head into their carapace by means of an S-shaped bend in the vertebral column. In the case of the sidenecks, the neck cannot be bent in the aforementioned S-shaped fashion and thus must be tucked along the sides.

Since turtles are unable to expand their chests, they have developed a unique means of respiration. There are special abdominal muscles inside the shell that work in conjunction

Turtles don't have teeth but instead have a powerful sharp-edged "beak" that enables them to slice through tough food items, including the hard shells of many snails and crustaceans. Keep this in mind when handling particularly large specimens. Photo of an albino Red-eared Slider, *Trachemys scripta elegans*, by Jim Merli.

Above: Most land turtles have high-domed shells, making it difficult for predators to get a grasp on them. Many also have the ability to withdraw into their shells and close up completely. Photo of two Desert Box Turtles, *Terrapene ornata luteola*, by K. H. Switak.

"The anatomy of a turtle usually has some relation to its habitat and the way in which it gets its food."

Below: Aquatic turtles usually have sleek low-domed shells, making it easy for them to swim. If they had the high-domed shells of their terrestrial counterparts, moving through the water would be much more difficult for them. Photo of a Spiny Softshell, *Trionyx spiniferus*, by W. P. Mara.

Many turtles can be sexually distinguished by the shape of their plastrons. Those of the males often are concave (inward curving, making it easier for them to mount a female during copulation), whereas those of the females are flat. Photo of a Striped Mud Turtle, *Kinosternon bauri*, by Isabelle Francais.

It is important to know what kind of habitat a turtle comes from before attempting to keep it in captivity. This Spotted Turtle, *Clemmys guttata*, for example, is a bog, swamp, and marshy meadow dweller, so it will need a fairly damp substrate and a large water body. Photo by Mella Panzella.

HOME SWEET HOME

Housing Your Turtles

Before acquiring any turtles, it is important to know what sort of habitat the species you're getting is accustomed to. After that you have to prepare the accommodations accordingly. Never buy a turtle first and then start worrying where you're going to house it! Your best bet is to read up on the natural history (particularly the habitat) of the species you intend to keep.

There are turtle species that are almost wholly aquatic, turtles that are semi-aquatic, and turtles that are wholly terrestrial. The kind of housing you can afford and the amount of space you can provide also will influence your decisions. It would be a mistake, for example, to consider keeping a large tortoise in an uptown apartment! There are, however, many small aquatic and terrestrial turtles that can be kept in a relatively small enclosure in your den or living room.

HOUSING AQUATIC TURTLES

The simplest kind of housing for aquatic turtles is the glass or acrylic tank normally used to keep pet fish. Although very young turtles can be kept in a relatively small tank, it is best to buy as large a tank as possible since turtles, of

Most land turtles want plenty of space, so it is best that you keep them outdoors. If you live in a temperate zone, keep them in a large heated room during the colder months. Adult land turtles confined to glass tanks usually do poorly, refusing food and quickly withering away. Photo of a Galapagos Tortoise, *Geochelone nigra*, by Isabelle Francais.

course, eventually will grow up.

The best kind of tank for turtles is the all-glass model, which can be purchased at your local pet shop. If you

have any kind of odd exacting requirements concerning the tank's shape or size, it is possible to have a manufacturer make one to your specifications (although this naturally will be rather costly).

While many wild turtles live in muddy bottomed watercourses, it is not a good idea for a keeper to use mud as a substrate. Since aquatic turtles swim around so much, the water always will be cloudy. A reasonable compromise is fine aquarium gravel, which is quite attractive and is easy to clean.

Since aquatic turtles are such filthy creatures, their water will need frequent changing. The problem with this is such disturbances can have a traumatic effect on the inmates. A far better idea is to install a filter, which will greatly reduce the number of complete water changes required.

Undergravel filters really

Changing the water in an aquatic turtle's tank can be a laborious chore, but it must be done. Make this task easier on yourself by obtaining an automatic water changer. You won't have to do much more than hook up the hose! Photo courtesy of Aquarium Products.

aren't suitable because captive aquatic turtles continually stir up their substrate. A much better option is an external canister filter. These operate out of the water and are known for their efficiency (not to mention their quietness). They can be maintenanced easily enough because you don't have to place your hands in the tank itself. Some canister filters are rather expensive, but they are well worth it. Your pet shop manager will be able to show you a range of models to choose from. And remember—*always* read the manufacturer's instructions

and recommendations before making a purchase!

Regardless of how efficient your filter is, you still should change at least some of the water every week. This is accomplished by bailing out (or siphoning) about a quarter of it with a jug or similar container and then replacing it with fresh water. Make sure the "new" water is of the same (or close to the same) temperature as the old, or the turtles may suffer some kind of shock.

About once per month, the water should be changed completely. During this time you will have to place the turtles in a holding container. The gravel should be removed and placed in a bucket so the tank interior can be thoroughly cleaned and rinsed. It is a good idea to have a spare stock of clean gravel handy for instant use, thus keeping the amount of time the turtles are out of

their home to a minimum. The dirty gravel can be sanitized with water from a garden hose, some kitchen soap, and a small amount of bleach. Remember to rinse it very thoroughly so no bleach residue remains. Basking rocks also should be washed during this time.

Even for highly aquatic turtles, a land area of some sort should be provided. You can divide a glass aquarium into two sections by fixing a sheet of glass or reasonably thick plexiglas (with the aid of some sort of waterproof sealant) at a diagonal angle somewhere near the aquarium's center. To one side of the sheet is the "land" area, which is filled with gravel and rocks. The other side is bedded with a shallow layer of gravel and filled with water, this of course being the swimming area. Make sure the turtles have easy access to a from each section

When you clean an aquatic turtle's enclosure, you also might want to clean the turtle itself. A simple warm-water-and-soft-sponge bath will remove most developing shell funguses, which in turn will help sidestep future health problems. Photo of a Yellow-spotted River Turtle, *Podocnemis unifilis*, by Isabelle Francais.

(a "staircase" of piled rocks in the water section is ideal). Also, if possible, it would be useful to have a drain at the bottom of the land area so excess water doesn't get the chance to accumulate.

HOUSING LAND TURTLES

Many tortoise and box turtle species require indoor housing with a large land area and a shallow water container. Very young specimens can be kept in a glass aquarium, with a paper towel substrate for easy cleaning. For a more attractive display, clean gravel can be used as the substrate. A waterbowl can be sunk into the gravel so the animals have easy access to it. Remember that the water needs to be very shallow or a small specimen very easily could drown.

Larger specimens must be kept in a spacious accommodation. This can consist either of a very large

Placing a full-spectrum bulb this close to your turtles may be bad for their vision. A height of one to two feet is more reasonable. Photo of newborn Red-footed Tortoises, *Geochelone carbonaria*, by Isabelle Francais.

aquarium or something called a "tortoise table." The latter strictly is a homemade accommodation that requires a bit of time, patience, and

carpentry skill to build.

First, you need a table. Obviously, it should be one you can spare, and it should be very sturdy. You may be able to buy a large second-hand model from a junk shop. The sides of the table (which will be the "walls" to the turtles) should consist of planks at least 12 in/30 cm high. You can attach these "walls" permanently to three sides of the table, then render the fourth removable to facilitate cleaning. The setup should be bedded with gravel and decorated with potted plants and large rocks. Be careful not to place any rocks or similar items near the "walls" or your pets may, in their attempt to escape, fall to the floor and injure themselves. Waterpools can be created simply by cutting out sections of the table surface and dropping in shallow pans.

Don't place a full-spectrum bulb over a screen unless absolutely necessary. Screens will filter out much of the light's beneficial qualities. Remember, direct light is best. Photo by Isabelle Francais.

Keeping an eye on the ambient heat and humidity of a turtle's enclosure is an important facet of good husbandry. Many land turtles need to be kept in a relatively dry environment, and land turtles that are kept too cold probably won't eat. Photo courtesy of Ocean Nutrition.

models available and, like the submersible heaters, can be purchased at most any pet shop. You may have to spend a little time fooling and fiddling with the lamp you buy in order to get the temperature of the basking spot just right. Bulb wattage will have an effect on this, as will distance from the lamp to the basking spot surface. Also note that the lamp should be suspended at only one end of the enclosure so a heat gradation is created. This way the inmates have a choice of temperature zones.

With regard to lighting, most turtles will be happy with 12 hours of light per day. The best kind of indoor lighting for turtles is called "full-spectrum" lighting. In short, this is a form of light that replicates the light given

Large aquatic turtles should be kept in very large tanks. Keeping such animals in relatively small enclosures not only is poor turtle keeping, it is cruel. Photo of a Florida East Coast Diamondback Terrapin, *Malaclemys terrapin tequesta*, by Aaron Norman.

off by the sun, which turtles need in order to survive. Your pet shop should offer bulbs that produce full-spectrum light (although such bulbs often are quite expensive). Always read over all manufacturer's instructions before putting the bulb to use.

HEATING AND LIGHTING

All turtles kept indoors must have supplementary heat and light to make up for the sunlight they would be exposed to if they were in the wild.

For heating aquatic turtles, you should maintain the water temperature at about 75°F/24°C, which easily can be accomplished through the use of a fully submersible aquarium heater, available at most any pet shop. For land-dwelling turtles (and aquatic turtles when they are basking), heat lamps are ideal. There are several

Undertank heating pads work well with turtles, particularly land turtles. A keeper can warm one particular section of an enclosure and leave the rest unwarmed, giving the inmates a choice of temperature zones. Photo courtesy of Fluker Farms.

OUTDOOR ACCOMMODATIONS

Most turtles can be kept outdoors in a pen or a walled-in garden. Even tropical species can be kept outside during the warmer parts of the year. Outdoor turtles often have an air of good health about them that indoor specimens rarely display. It undoubtedly is the fresh air and sunshine that at least partially causes this.

Aquatic turtles will, of course, need a suitably sized pool. Such a pool can range from a baby's wading pool to a full-scale water garden. Whatever the case, the area around the pool must be fenced- or walled-in to prevent your turtles from wandering. Many people have acquired somebody else's pet turtle this way! The boundaries can be as simple as a wire-net fence (which should be buried about 12 in/30 cm underground to prevent the turtles from digging their way out) or as substantial as a brick wall (again, buried deep). If you intend to keep aquatic and land turtles together, you must ensure that the pool has gently sloping sides so the land turtles easily can get out if they fall in.

Apart from the fresh air and the sunshine, another great advantage to outdoor

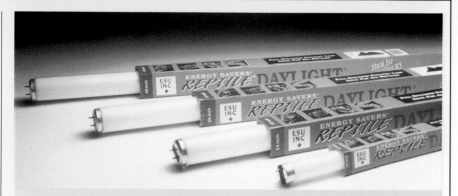

Providing turtles with the correct photoperiod (day/night cycle) and quality of light is very important. Both are factors in determining their behaviorisms as well as maintaining their health. Bulbs designed specifically for the keeping of reptiles and amphibians are available at many pet shops. Photo courtesy of Coralife/Energy Savers.

pens is that your turtles will find some of their own food. Aquatic turtles will benefit from the various insects that turn up in a pool, while your land turtles will be able to forage for the fresh veggies you've planted for them. You should keep the area inside the enclosure planted with a

mixture of weed and vegetable seeds. A good idea is to have two fenced-off areas within the pen and use them alternatively, opening one when the greens are mature, and then replanting it while your turtles feed on the contents of the other.

Land turtles kept outdoors all year long in temperate climates must have a place to hibernate when winter comes. Such an area can consist of an enclosed waterproof hut with a small access door. The hut can be loosely packed with straw, with more straw being packed over the roof and sides as the weather gets colder. Aquatic turtles may hibernate in the mud at the bottom of the pool or burrow into the soil elsewhere. It is advised that you place piles of straw or mulch in various spots in order to give them a choice of sites.

Many turtles can be kept in something known as an *aquaterrarium*, which essentially is an enclosure setup that has equal (or nearly equal) land and water bodies. Aquaterrariums are ideal for turtles that spend a lot of time basking. Photo of Pan's Box Turtle, *Cuora pani*, by Isabelle Francais.

MEALTIME!

The Diet of Turtles and Tortoises

Whether you're a person or a pig, an ant or an aardvark, or a turtle or a tortoise, you *must* have a balanced diet in order to survive. Since animals live in different habitats and eat different things, they obtain their balanced diets in different ways. They have, after all, spent millions of years working on the problem. The notion is that animals and their diets are ecologically linked, and it applies to turtles and tortoises as much as does any other creatures. There are species that eat just about anything, and then there are those that have a very specialized diet (example—some marine turtles have a staple diet of jellyfish). Whatever the case may be, a turtle knows what it needs to survive, and more importantly, how to get it.

In general, most of the aquatic turtle species we keep as pets are carnivorous, while most of the terrestrial species are largely herbivorous. We can ensure that our pet turtles get a balanced diet by giving them as many different legitimate food items as possible and further offer a vitamin/mineral supplement at regular intervals. All turtles should be fed on a daily basis, or every other day at least. Uneaten food should be removed and

Many land turtles accept fruits like the banana being taken by this handsome *Geochelone* sp. Turtles that accept only plant material are known as *herbivores*, whereas those that take only animal material are called *carnivores*. Photo by Susan C. Miller.

disposed of before it spoils (and, with aquatic species, spoils the water).

The following is a discussion of some of the foods that can be given to turtles and tortoises.

ANIMAL MATERIAL

Many carnivorous turtles will eagerly devour strips of raw lean beef or other meat. There certainly is nothing wrong with giving your turtles raw meat, but only as a supplement or a treat since it does not contain all of the required nutrients.

Most aquatic turtles will accept a variety of invertebrates. These include aquatic insect larvae, aquatic worms, snails, and crustaceans such as freshwater shrimp and crayfish. By turning over flat stones in a shallow watercourse you should be able to catch a number of items, especially if you use a small net.

A good substitute for captured aquatic livefood can be found in your local seafood market (or supermarket that sells fresh seafood). Shrimp will be taken, shell and all, by most aquatic turtles, as will the meat of crab, lobster, mussels, oysters, scallops, etc. Saltwater items should be thoroughly washed in freshwater to remove any excess salt. Since these items often are rather expensive,

Bloodworms are a favorite food of many aquatic turtles, particularly young specimens. They can be purchased at many pet shops, usually in both alive and frozen form. Photo courtesy of Hikari.

It is advised that you use a calcium supplement with all your turtles. This will promote correct bone growth and decrease the likelihood of soft shell. Photo courtesy of American Reptile.

you may want to offer them only as an occasional treat. Strips of fish or small whole fish also can be given on a regular basis. Freshwater fish are preferable, and if you live near a trout farm or similar you may be able to buy juvenile trout on a regular basis.

You also can find many suitable food items in your garden (if you have one, that is). Garden snails can be found in moist and dark areas. Earthworms are another highly nutritious food. You can dig them up from damp soil, wash them free of dirt, and feed them straight to your turtles. If you dig worms out of a compost heap, keep them in a bucket of moist and sterile potting soil for a day or two so they can pass any potentially unhealthy material from their system.

If you need a lot of earthworms, it may be worthwhile setting up an "earthworm collecting station." You can do this

simply by "turning" a couple of square yards of soil where you know worms to be, then covering the turned area with a 2 in/5 cm layer of dead leaves, grass clippings, and straw or hay. Wet the

Freeze-dried mealworms should be accepted by most captive carnivorous turtles, particularly aquatic specimens that have become accustomed to captive living. Photo courtesy of Fluker Farms.

area thoroughly, then cover it with old sacks or other cloth material, making sure to also moisten this material regularly. After about ten days, you'll be able to collect the worms that have congregated underneath. A worm station can be used for several months, and if you set up two stations you probably won't run out of worms.

By searching under logs, stones, and so forth you will be able to find a number of other food items, including spiders, pillbugs, beetles, and slugs. If you don't like touching these creatures you can scoop them into a jar or plastic container via the lid.

There are some commercially available livefoods that will come in useful. These include mealworms, crickets, locusts, and waxworms. Most can be successfully propagated in the home, but if you have only a small number of turtles it is natural foods.

PLANT MATTER

As we have discussed, land tortoises are largely herbivorous. In the wild they feed on a variety of vegetation found in their area. Since you probably won't have stocks of the exact same plants found in their wild habitats, you must substitute them with a variety of greens, fruits, and vegetables. Most land tortoises can be given a daily dish of mixed salad. Include such items as lettuce, cabbage, broccoli, grated root vegetables (carrots, turnips, parsnips), tomatoes, cucumbers, apples, pears, bananas, peaches, and so on.

VITAMIN/MINERAL SUPPLEMENTS

Turtles, especially young specimens, will develop deformed shells and other abnormalities if their diets

When maintaining crickets as turtle food, give them a high-calcium diet so they'll be more nutritious. This technique often is called "gut-loading." High-calcium cricket foods can be purchased at many pet shops. Photo courtesy of Fluker Farms.

perhaps best just to purchase a few items from your local pet shop when you need them.

Specially formulated dry foods now are available. These include floating sticks and pellets and offer a balanced meal in themselves. Check with your pet shop to see what's available. Although these foods are very nutritious, they should make up no more than 50% of a captive turtle's diet, the remainder consisting of a variety of

Some pet shops carry dry foods that are specially formulated for tortoises. Such foods not only provide a tortoise with plenty of nutrition, they also are easy to store and portion out. Photo courtesy of Ocean Nutrition.

are inadequate. Although a wide variety of foods probably will be adequate, you still should offer a regular dose of micronutrients. You can buy multivitamin/mineral supplements in your pet shop. They come in both powder and liquid form, but the former is preferable. Powdered supplements can be sprinkled over the mixed foods of vegetarian species or can be scoured into strips of lean meat or fish, then fed directly to your pets.

There now are quite a few commercially produced food items for aquatic turtles. They are available in a variety of sizes and can be purchased at many pet shops. Photo courtesy of Wardley.

Strips of meat will be taken with great eagerness by most carnivorous turtles but should be offered only sparingly since they often have a high content of both salt and fat. Turtles shown are adult Red-eared Sliders, *Trachemys scripta elegans*. Photo by Susan C. Miller.

Cactus fruits are a popular food item of desert-dwelling species but may be hard for the average keeper to acquire. Nevertheless, if you have the opportunity to offer them, do so. Photo of an Ornate Box Turtle, *Terrapene ornata*, by Mella Panzella.

Most turtles love iceberg lettuce. In spite of this, it should *not* be given because it has virtually no nutritional value. Romaine lettuce is much better for them and should be accepted with equal enthusiasm. Photo of a young Eastern Box Turtle, *Terrapene carolina*, by W. P. Mara.

"Turtles...will develop deformed shells and other abnormalities if their diets are inadequate."

Mealworms can be maintained in captivity for quite some time. A plastic shoebox like the one shown will take care of the housing. Fill it with some grain or bran and add in a few fruit slices. Mealworms are an excellent supplementary food item for turtles but should not be used as a staple because they are not nutritionally complete. Photo by Isabelle Francais.

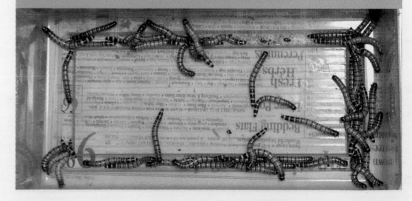

MAKING MORE TURTLES

Reproduction and Captive Breeding

Since many turtle species are becoming scarce in the wild, it is important that hobbyists breed their captives whenever possible. Consider that each turtle bred in captivity means one less taken from the wild. There is the possibility that some species one day may exist only in captivity, but then survival in captivity is better than no survival at all.

It is with these points in mind that I stress the importance of captive breeding. Although it's nice to have a single turtle as a pet, you surely will have much greater pleasure if you obtain a pair and breed them.

SEPARATING THE BOYS FROM THE GIRLS

Differences between males and females varies from species to species. In some it is rather difficult to distinguish the sexes, whereas in others it is relatively easy. In most of the species regularly kept as pets, the plastron of the female either is flat, or convex (outwardly rounded),

while the male's plastron is concave (inwardly rounded), making it a little easier for him to stay on top of the female during copulation. Male turtles of most species have long and thick tails that extend well beyond the carapace margin, while those of the female are relatively short and slight, rarely extending more than a

Anyone who owns adult male/female pairs of turtles is strongly urged to breed them. In an age when the future of many species is so uncertain, captive propagation may be the only alternative to extinction. Photo of a breeding pair of Spur-thighed Tortoises, *Geochelone sulcata*, by K. H. Switak.

few millimeters from the carapace margin.

In some aquatic turtles, the male has exceptionally long front claws, which he uses to

stroke his mate during courtship. Also, the adult female may be considerably larger than the male.

ENCOURAGING THEM TO BREED

In the wild, turtles are influenced to breed through certain climatic conditions. Particulars will vary from species to species (area to area), but generally speaking most turtles become ready to breed after the winter, when warmer weather is on its way. Many temperate and subtropical species hibernate during the winter. Hibernation plays an important role in the breeding cycle. Specimens kept out of hibernation still might breed, but rarely will any fertile eggs be produced. Also, remember that only turtles in peak health should be hibernated because sick or malnourished specimens will not be able to withstand the inherent rigors of the hibernation process.

Even if you don't allow your

indoor turtles to experience a "full" term of hibernation, you still can give them a winter "rest period," this being milder than actual hibernation. Eight weeks at reduced temperature and photoperiod should do the trick for most temperate or subtropical species. Details are as follows—reduce the temperature gradually over a week at the end of November until it's around 59°F/15°C. At the same time, reduce your turtles' photoperiod to about six to eight hours per day and stop feeding them. Keep them cool for about eight weeks, and then, at the end of January, you can start raising their temperature again, gradually, until it's back to its original, "active season" level. Provide basking facilities, increase photoperiod, and

Most tortoises grow slowly and will not reach sexual maturity for some time, so if you're planning on breeding them, perhaps you'll want to consider purchasing adults from the start. Photo of three young Leopard Tortoises, *Geochelone pardalis*, by W. P. Mara.

start offering food again. Sometimes this kind of "compromise hibernation" is enough to bring turtles into breeding condition.

Turtles kept in outdoor accommodations will hibernate naturally, but you must provide them with suitable places such as piles of straw or mulch placed over soft earth or sand. Land tortoises can be provided with little "huts" stuffed with straw or hay. As the weather grows colder, more straw and/or hay can be piled on top of the hut. Hibernaculi should be sheltered from cold winds and rain. A sheet of corrugated iron or similar, placed over the hibernation heap and weighted down with heavy rocks, should keep things dry.

Tropical turtles do not require a period of hibernation to bring them into breeding condition, but instead they often are stimulated by the onset of summer rains. Temperature can be reduced by five degrees and photoperiod reduced to ten hours per day for a period of one month in the winter. Feedings also should be reduced slightly.

After the one-month period, temperature, photoperiod, and feedings all should be raised back to their normal levels. At

Before you can breed turtles, you naturally have to have a male and a female! Characteristics that tell them apart include the concave plastron of the most males (as opposed to the flat plastron of most females), and the long and thick tail on the males as opposed to a short and slender tail on the females. Photo of the posterior end of a Red-eared Slider, *Trachemys scripta elegans*, by Maleta and Jerry G. Walls.

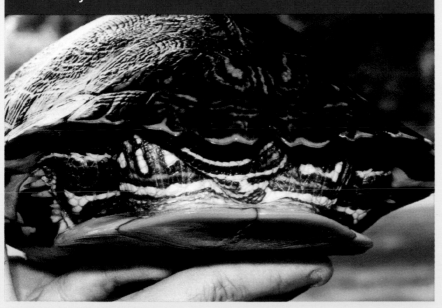

the same time, in the case of tropical land tortoises, the humidity in the terrarium should be increased. This can be done by spraying the interior of the enclosure two or three times per day. For aquatic turtles, artificial rainfall created by using recirculated water from the water body may be provide stimulus for breeding.

Climatic influences cause a buildup of sex hormones, and in turn ignite sexual activity. In land tortoises, the amorous male chases a female and butts her with his shell, sometimes biting her on the limbs and head. Such activity may appear quite violent but is quite natural. A receptive female eventually remains still and allows the male to clamber onto her carapace from the rear. Aquatic turtles usually mate in the water, often coming up for air several times during copulation,

Newborn turtles should be given food at least every other day. Particular attention should be given to their calcium intake since they are so susceptible to soft-shell disease. Photo of a normally colored Red-eared Slider, *Trachemys scripta elegans*, by W. P. Mara

The tireless efforts of captive breeders worldwide have given the herpetocultural hobby some stunning turtle specimens, including the ever-popular "pastel" Red-eared Slider, *Trachemys scripta elegans*. Photo by W. P. Mara.

which may last from five minutes to a full hour.

EGGLAYING

All turtles lay their eggs on land. In the case of some aquatic species, egglaying is the only time they leave the water. Most species excavate a nest hole in the substrate with their hind limbs, though a few lay under piles of decaying vegetation. The eggs are carefully covered and camouflaged with earth or vegetation before they are abandoned. Clutch sizes vary from species to species, but in the case of most commonly kept species it ranges from about two to 16.

Incubation takes about 50 to 70 days with most temperate species. With some tropical species it can take as long as 150 days. There is very little parental care among turtles;

the eggs are left to hatch on their own. Hatchling turtles are most vulnerable to predators. This applies especially to hatchling aquatic turtles, who may have to cross wide areas of open ground in order to reach the relative safety of the water.

ARTIFICIAL INCUBATION

Since most captive turtles are not given the ideal surroundings for egglaying, eggs often are deposited haphazardly on the substrate or in the water bath. If you suspect any of your turtles to be gravid, provide them with a deep dish of moist sand. Once the eggs have been laid, you will have to remove them for artificial incubation. Unless you live in a suitable climate, even eggs laid by turtles kept in an outdoor walled pen must be carefully dug out and placed in an incubator, which

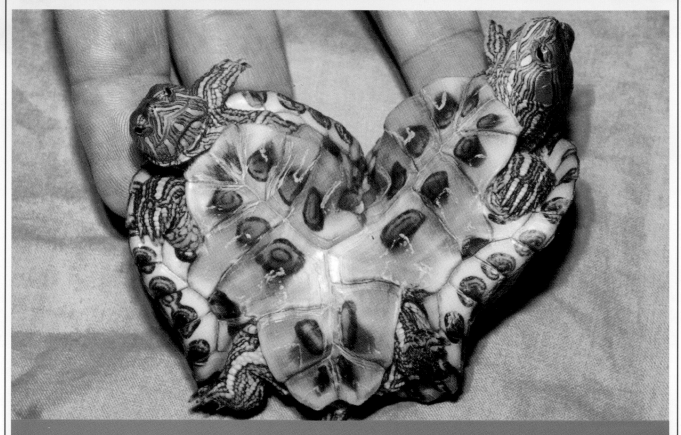

Although fascinating to see, siamese turtle specimens usually have a difficult time surviving and probably should be euthanized. Specimens joined only at the neck (two heads, one body) might have a fighting chance at a "normal" life, but those that are connected in odd places, like the Red-eared Slider, *Trachemys scripta elegans*, shown here, usually don't live long. Photo by W. P. Mara.

often is nothing more than a plastic container bedded with some type of moisture-retaining substrate and topped with an aerated lid.

The eggs should be situated in the exact same position in which they were laid, and their "top" marked with a non-toxic marker. A versatile incubation medium that has been used very successfully is vermiculite, which is a sterile and inert granular material often used in horticulture. Large-grade vermiculite is best and

Notice the egg tooth on this neonatal slider, *Pseudemys* sp. It enables the turtle to cut through its shell when hatching. (Also notice the aberrant pattern, which is what made precise species identification so difficult). Photo by W. P. Mara.

should be watered until moist (not soggy).

The eggs should be buried so only their top third is exposed. The incubation temperature should be somewhere around 77 and 86°F/25 and 30°C. Check the eggs daily, and be sure the vermiculite doesn't dry out. You spray the vermiculite if it starts to dry, but be sure not to spray the eggs in the process.

Length of incubation varies from species to species, but most should hatch within 65 to 90 days.

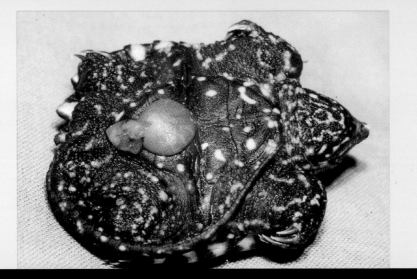

Above: Detail of a newborn Snapping Turtle, *Chelydra serpentina*, with the yolk sac still attached. This sac will continue to feed the turtle for a few days then will be resorbed. Photo by W. P. Mara.

Below: Once the yolk sac is gone, a small crack will be visible. In time, however, this too will disappear. Photo of a neonatal Blanding's Turtle, *Emydoidea blandingi*, by W. P. Mara.

Turtle eggs can be hibernated much in the same way that many snake eggs can—partially buried in a bedding of moist vermiculite and draped with moistened sphagnum moss. This is the egg of a Snapping Turtle, *Chelydra serpentina*. Photo by W. P. Mara.

"Newborns should be raised on a balanced and varied diet."

Hatchling turtles may be quite shy and remain in their shells for some time. If this happens, don't force them to come out. Instead, give them increased privacy. As soon as they feel safe, they'll expose themselves. Photo of a hatchling Pancake Tortoise, *Malacochersus tornieri*, by Paul Freed.

Sea turtles were shamelessly exploited for years, but now many captive-breeding projects are well underway thanks to the dedication of many conservationists. Shown is a nursery setup in the South Pacific, and the turtle in the foreground is a Green Turtle, *Chelonia mydas*. Photo by Zoltan Takacs.

Neonatal turtles should be housed in their own "nursery" enclosures rather than with their parents. Not only do the parents have no parental care instincts to speak of, they may inadvertently take bites out of their own young! Photo of two hatching Eastern Painted Turtles, *Chrysemys picta picta*, by Mella Panzella.

HATCHING AND REARING

When ready to hatch, a young turtle slits open its shell with a special "egg tooth" located at the front of its snout. The tooth is then shed shortly after hatching. The yolk sac will still be attached to the plastron of the hatchling; do not attempt to remove this! Allow the turtle to gradually absorb its contents and the membrane will then dry up and fall off in a day or two.

Newborn turtles should be placed in a nursery enclosure set up appropriately for whatever species is being housed. Do not house neonates with adults because the latter

Albino turtles always are likely to raise eyebrows, especially when they're as stunning as the albino Red-ears, *Trachemys scripta elegans*. Albino Red-ears are regularly bred in captivity and can be obtained by any hobbyist willing to spend a little extra money. Photo by R. D. Bartlett.

may take nips at the former. Newborns should be raised on a balanced and varied diet. Offer a variety of invertebrate foods for hatchling aquatic turtles, including tubifex worms, mosquito larvae, small crustaceans, small mealworms, and so on. As a treat, you also can give small pieces of lean meat, ox heart, and cooked chicken. Herbivorous species can be given finely chopped fruits and vegetables. Finally, it is recommended that a regular vitamin/supplement be added to the diet of *all* newborn turtles.

After you've had some experience breeding common turtle species, you might want to try breeding some of the rarer ones. If so, make sure you contact the proper governmental agencies and obtain the necessary permits. Keeping animals illegally is a good way to get yourself into a lot of trouble. Photo by U. E. Friese.

One attractive aspect of breeding turtles is that you can sell the offspring or even trade them for species you don't have, thus expanding your collection. Photo of a Red-footed Tortoise, *Geochelone carbonaria*, by R. D. Bartlett.

TURN YOUR HEAD AND COUGH

Health Problems of Captive Turtles

When deciding to keep a turtle as a pet, one of the last things you may have in mind is the possibility that it will get sick. Turtles are remarkably resistant to diseases when kept in optimum conditions. On the other hand, prolonged exposure to unsuitable conditions will cause great amounts of stress, this being followed by a reduction in the aforementioned disease resistance.

One of the most important aspects of keeping your turtles healthy is *cleanliness*. In the wild, decaying fecal matter is quickly disposed of by the processes nature. Captive animals, however, often are kept in conditions where such matter will remain in the one spot and continue to build up until the keeper (you) removes it.

CHOOSING YOUR STOCK

In order to minimize the possibility of disease, you should make every effort to ensure that the specimens you acquire are in good health to begin with. This process will start at the pet shop—you should not purchase specimens from premises that are dirty or smelly, or where the turtles are kept in unclean and overcrowded enclosures. Dealers who obviously go out of their way to care for and display their turtles are most desirable.

Once you've chosen a dealer, your next task is to ensure that the turtle you intend to purchase is as healthy as possible. Always choose alert specimens, for ill specimens often are listless and lethargic. Ensure that the shell is in good shape, i.e., has no cracks or signs of abnormal growth. Check the head, neck, and

Aquatic turtles are particularly difficult to keep healthy because they're remarkably filthy, constantly defecating in their water. Thus, the keeper has to be particularly diligent and disciplined when it comes to cleaning. Prevention of disease is much easier than cure. Photo of a False Map Turtle, *Graptemys pseudogeographica*, by K. T. Nemuras.

limbs for signs of injury, infection, or for infestations of mites or ticks. Never select specimens that feel too "light" in relation to their size. Inspect the mouth, nostrils, and vent for signs of inflammation or runny discharge. Ask the

dealer if the turtle is eating and what food it's taking. An easy feeding test is simply to ask if you can see the animal eat. Make your final decision only when you feel sure of the animal's health.

HANDLING

In general, turtles should not be handled any more than necessary. Turtles are pets to be studied and admired rather than stroked and cuddled. However, it may be necessary to handle your turtles at various times such as during cleaning, for health inspections, or to apply treatments.

Most pet turtles respond reasonably well to handling. Land tortoises in particular are very docile and usually withdraw into their shells if picked up. On the other hand, many aquatic turtles will struggle, and since they are quite slippery, you need to use both hands to get a firm grip on the shell. It always is best to hold a turtle over a sturdy surface so that if you drop it it won't fall far. A turtle dropped onto a hard floor from a good height could be severely injured.

Some turtles, especially snappers and softshells, rarely tame and often will lunge at you. Large specimens even have been known to remove fingers and toes! Thus, when in close quarters with such specimens, caution is the order of the day.

Bringing a sick turtle to a vet is never a pleasant affair, but it is better than trying to treat the animal on your own. If you're not a professional vet, don't pretend otherwise. Many procedures are just too complicated to try at home. Photo of a Red-footed Tortoise, *Geochelone carbonaria*, receiving an injection, by Dr. Fredric L. Frye in *Reptile Care*.

"Many new specimens may look perfectly healthy, but it is best to keep them separate from your existing stock."

Newborn turtles are particularly susceptible to disease, so it is vital that a keeper be particularly valiant with the animal's husbandry. Once through the first two years of life, a turtle's chances of survival are quite good (with continuing top-notch care, of course). Photo of a Wood Turtle, *Clemmys insculpta*, by K. T. Nemuras.

QUARANTINE

Many new specimens may *look* perfectly healthy, but to be on the safe side, it is best to keep them separate from your existing stock until you're sure the newcomers aren't harboring any contagious diseases. New turtles should be placed in a quarantine enclosure with only the most basic furnishings. Keep a close watch on them for 21 days, and if no disease symptoms appear during this time you can be more or less assured that they are healthy.

PROBLEMS AND SOLUTIONS

Prevention of disease primarily lies with the practice of good husbandry. Turtles kept in optimum conditions, not subjected to extreme stress, and provided with a balanced diet normally will stay healthy for years. However, the occasional

Once into the later stages, shell problems can spell death for a turtle. Here, for example, is a case of shell rot that is so severe, the animal (an Eastern Painted Turtle, *Chrysemys picta picta*) lived for only a few weeks after the photo was taken. Photo by W. P. Mara.

Minor cuts and abrasions often can be treated with hydrogen peroxide and/or a variety of antibiotic creams, but severe wounds like this one really should be examined by a professional. Photo by Dr. Fredric L. Frye in *Reptile Care*.

ailment still surfaces, and it is wise to know what to do in such cases. The following paragraphs deal with some of the more common problems encountered by captive turtles, and what a keeper can do about them.

Malnutrition: Prolonged deficiencies of certain nutrients can result in various problems, including abnormal shell and bone growth, inflamed eyes, metabolic anomalies, and so on. These conditions will be avoided if you simply keep your turtles on a balanced diet. In severe cases of malnutrition, your veterinarian may be able to help with a regime of vitamin injections.

External Parasites: The parasites most commonly found on captive turtles probably are mites and ticks (although wild-caught aquatic specimens often have leeches attached). Mites can multiply into huge numbers if undetected, causing the turtle to suffer skin irritation, loss of appetite, anemia, and other stress-causing conditions. Mites are less than the size of a pinhead and hide during the day. When dealing with a full-blown infestation, remove the turtles from their enclosure and bathe them in lukewarm water containing a mild antiseptic (povidone-iodine for example). The original enclosure should be stripped and cleaned with water, soap, and bleach. Surrounding areas can be treated using a mild insecticide spray, but at no time should the spray come into contact with your turtles.

Ticks usually are present on turtles that were recently captured. They may be up to 0.25 in/6 mm in length and will attach themselves with their sucking mouthparts, often remaining in the same spot for days or even weeks. They usually conceal themselves in places such as skin folds on the neck or at the base of the hind limbs, but they also have been known to latch onto the joints between scutes. Before you remove a tick, dab it with alcohol to relax it. Then you can twist it out using your thumb and forefinger. When in doubt, always consult a veterinarian.

Worm Infestations: Worms often are present in the alimentary tract of turtles. Infestations should be treated with a vermicide via food or, in severe cases, administered with a stomach tube. Ask your veterinarian for advice on this.

Bacterial and Protozoan

Infections: These are likely to occur in turtles living in unhygienic conditions. They include various enteric diseases such as salmonellosis (which can also be transmitted to man, so personal hygiene is also very important to the turtle handler!) and dysentery. Symptoms an infected turtle may show include foul-smelling or watery diarrhea, loss of appetite, and lethargy. In such cases you immediately should consult a veterinarian.

Fungal Infections: These usually occur on aquatic turtles or land turtles kept in an environment that is too moist. In severe cases, the fungus gets right under the scutes, causing the victim to shed prematurely. There are several proprietary fungicides available, but before using any you should talk to your veterinarian.

Respiratory Infections: These fortunately are uncommon in turtles, but when they do occur they can be dangerous if left untreated. Symptoms include

One of the obvious early signs of respiratory disease in aquatic turtles is the appearance of tiny bubbles from the mouth and nostrils. It is sensible to run monthly health checks on all your specimens in order to catch diseases in their earliest stages. Photo of a Painted Turtle, *Chrysemys picta*, by Dr. Fredric L. Frye in *Reptile Care*.

labored breathing and discharge from the nostrils (or a blockage of the same). The good news is such infections often respond to antibiotic treatment.

Cracks in a turtle's shell can be taken care of by a vet and often will heal with very little scarring. Untreated cracks may still heal, but the scarring will be quite ugly. Photo by W. P. Mara.

LIVING IN WATERWORLD

Aquatic Turtles Species

Many thousands of aquatic turtles are kept as pets. Hatchlings in particular seem to be immensely popular with both pros and beginners, probably because their keeping requirements are less demanding than those of adult specimens.

The turtle family Emydidae is the largest turtle family, containing about 85 species in 31 genera. Its members sometimes are referred to as the freshwater turtles. Many are medium-sized with a low-domed carapace. Some are attractively colored, making them desirable to hobbyists. They are found on every continent except Australia and Antarctica, and the North American species probably are the best known/ most studied. These include the sliders, cooters, paints, and maps. Although the majority of the turtles in this family are highly aquatic, some species occasionally will be found a good distance from water.

The **Red-eared Slider,** *Trachemys scripta elegans,* has been one of the most

The Red-eared Slider, *Trachemys scripta elegans*, is one the most popular turtles in the history of the herpetocultural hobby. Millions of specimens have been sold through pet shops worldwide, and there is some justification to this—Red-ears make superb pets. Photo by Isabelle Francais.

popular aquaterrarium subjects for decades. At one time it was commercially bred in large numbers and exported to many parts of the world. As the common name suggests, it has an attractive red patch on each side of its head. There are several other elegans subspecies, ranging throughout southeastern USA then moving south all the way down to Brazil. All make pretty good vivarium pets. They start off their lives being very carnivorous, but become more omnivorous as they mature.

The **Painted Turtle,** *Chrysemys picta,* is a small, attractive species that grows to about 8 in/20 cm. It ranges all across North America and has four subspecies. The general color is olive to black with yellow or red scute borders and yellow and/or red stripes on the neck, limbs, and tail. There is some color variation

The Painted Turtle, *Chrysemys picta*, makes a fine pet, feeding on a variety of invertebrates in its younger years and switching to a more omnivorous diet as it gets older. Photo by R. D. Bartlett.

The Spotted Turtle, *Clemmys guttata*, has a loyal following in the herpetocultural hobby. It makes a fine pet but is becoming rare in the wild. If you have a pair, try breeding them. Photo by Aaron Norman.

between the subspecies, and intergrades are common where the ranges overlap. Like *Trachemys scripta*, the young of *C. picta* are carnivorous, becoming more omnivorous as they age.

The **Spotted Turtle**, *Clemmys guttata*, is another small species, with a maximum adult length of about 5 in/12.5 cm. It also is one of the most attractive and sought-after emydid turtles in the world. The carapace is black and flecked with small yellow spots. There are further yellow to orange spots on the head, neck, and limbs. Ranging from the Great Lakes region south (along the Atlantic Coast) to northern Florida, it is an ideal subject for the outdoor pond because, given the right conditions, it will breed readily. It is mainly carnivorous, feeding on a variety of meat and invertebrates.

The **Chicken Turtle**, *Deirochelys reticularia*, is characterized by having a

"The Spotted Turtle is an ideal subject for the outdoor pond..."

particularly long neck. Growing to 10 in/25 cm, its rather plain olive-colored carapace is offset by the attractive green and yellow stripes on its neck and limbs. There are three subspecies, all native to the southeastern USA.

At one time this turtle was eaten by southerners and was said to have a chicken flavor, hence its common name. Specimens can be feisty and are capable of giving a hard bite. Due to the length of their neck, they must be handled cautiously. They are omnivorous, feeding on a wide variety of animal and vegetable materials.

Map turtles, genus *Graptemys*, of which there are several species, are so named because of the map-like pattern on their shells. The best known species is the **Common Map Turtle**, *Graptemys geographica*, the male of which grows to barely 6

The Chicken Turtle, *Deirochelys reticularia*, is not seen for sale as often as its close relatives the sliders and the cooters, but it is no less suitable as a pet. A native primarily of the U. S. Coastal Plain, it prefers still waters such as ponds and lakes and eats a wide variety of both animal and plant matter. Photo by W. P. Mara.

Most of the map turtles make good pets, but, like any other aquatic turtles, they are a headache to house and keep clean. However, their appetites are monstrous, which makes them easy to keep alive (as opposed to finicky specimens, who are a true nightmare). Photo by Isabelle Francais.

in/15 cm, and the female to almost twice that length! It is found in eastern central USA from the Great Lakes south to Tennessee and Alabama. Maps remain largely carnivorous throughout their lives.

One of the prettiest map turtles is the Yellow-blotched Map Turtle, *Graptemys flavimaculata*. It almost never turns up for sale, which is unfortunate for the keeper (not the turtles) since it supposedly makes a first-rate pet. Photo by K. T. Nemuras.

Blanding's Turtle, *Emydoidea blandingi*, is a very cold-tolerant creature, native to the Great lakes region of North America. Growing to a length of about 10 in/25 cm, it makes an ideal subject for the outdoor pond, feeding on a variety of animal material.

The **European Pond Terrapin,** *Emys orbicularis*, once was a very popular European pet and was widespread across most of Europe. Unfortunately it has become very scarce in the wild and thus is protected in most places. Nevertheless, it makes a hardy captive, and anyone who has a chance to breed it should do so.

Mud and musk turtles comprise the family Kinosternidae. There are four genera and about 23 species,

One of the most underrated aquatic turtles is the beautiful and fascinating Blanding's Turtle, *Emydoidea blandingi*. A native primarily of the Great Lakes region of the United States, it is a dedicated carnivore, taking a variety of both vertebrate and invertebrate food items. Photo by K. T. Nemuras.

One map turtle commonly seen in pet shops is the Mississippi Map, *Graptemys kohni* (considered by many to be *Graptemys pseudogeographica kohni*). Like most maps, it is a carnivore and, under ideal conditions, does well in captivity. Photo by Aaron Norman.

The **Eastern Mud Turtle**, *Kinosternon subrubrum*, still is fairly common in most of the southern United States and is a veteran captive. Barely reaching 5 in/12.5 cm, it more or less is uniformly colored in reddish brown to olive. The plastron is double hinged so the head and tail can be hidden when danger threatens. The Eastern Mud can be kept in a large aquaterrarium or an outdoor pond (in suitable areas). It is largely carnivorous.

The **Stinkpot Turtle**, *Sternotherus odoratus*, is the best known of the musk turtles. Like the other members of this family, it makes a relatively good pet and stops emitting musk once it becomes accustomed to handling. The smooth carapace normally is uniformly brown in color. There are two narrow white stripes on each side of the head and neck. Both the Stinkpot and the Eastern Mud do well in an aquaterrarium, feeding on a

Although the Stinkpot Turtle, *Sternotherus odoratus*, will emit a foul-smelling musk when first handled (hence its common name), it eventually calms down in captivity and loses this most unpleasant habit. Photo by Aaron Norman.

The European Pond Terrapin, *Emys orbicularis*, was at one time immensely popular in its native Europe. However, it has become quite rare in the wild and now is difficult to acquire. Photo by Hans Budde.

ranging from eastern Canada south to Argentina. All mud and musk turtles have a rather unpleasant defense mechanism—they emit a foul odor from their cloacal glands when disturbed. Fortunately, captive specimens drop this habit after a time.

The saddest part about the European Pond Terrapin becoming so rare is that it is a superb captive. Most specimens adapt quickly to captivity and can be expected to breed. Photo by Hands Budde.

variety of animal matter.

Though not really recommended for beginners, the two snapping turtles of the family Chelydridae are interesting enough to be

The Eastern Mud Turtle, *Kinosternon subrubrum*, can be housed in a largely aquatic setup and maintained on a carnivore's diet of earthworms and assorted insects with the occasional strip of raw lean beef. Photo by R. D. Bartlett.

Above: Rarer than rare—one of the few known albino specimens of the Eastern Mud Turtle, *Kinosternon subrubrum subrubrum*. Photo by R. D. Bartlett.

"Like the other members of this family, [the Stinkpot Turtle] makes a relatively good pet . . ."

Below: One of the prettier mud turtles is the Striped Mud Turtle, *Kinosternon bauri*. Unfortunately, it almost never turns up for sale. It is a native of the southeastern United States from South Carolina to the Lower Florida Keys. Photo by Aaron Norman.

Snapping Turtles are best purchased very small (hatchling size obviously is ideal). They are most manageable during their first few years, taking a variety of food items and requiring a relatively small enclosure. Photo by W. P. Mara.

Snapping Turtles spend virtually all of their time underwater, only coming on land to lay their eggs and (rarely) to bask. Thus, their enclosure setup should reflect their largely aquatic habits—a half-filled aquarium with one large exposed rock will be sufficient. Photo by R. T. Zappalorti.

of North America, Africa, and Asia. As their common name suggests, softshells lack the hard, scuted shell of most turtles, the scutes being replaced with a soft, leathery skin. Softshells are very aquatic, only coming on land to lay eggs. They have a long snout that enables them to stretch up for air without leaving the safety of the water. Softshells are almost entirely carnivorous. They can be kept in an aquarium with about 8 in/20 cm and a sandy substrate. Newborns need basking areas, for even though they belong to a highly aquatic family, they will grow tired from constantly swimming and need a place to rest.

The **Indian Flapshell Turtle,** *Lissemys punctata,* is difficult to obtain, but since it makes a good captive and is very attractive, it is worth a mention. Adults reach a maximum length of about 8 in/20 cm. Youngsters often are black with a sprinkling of large

This Alligator Snapping Turtle still bears the plastral split where the yolk sac was. This will heal relatively quickly, so don't be alarmed if you see it on any turtle's you've purchased. Photo by R. D. Bartlett.

Notice the little pink spot on the floor of this Alligator Snapping Turtle's mouth. It is part of the turtle's tongue and is used to lure fish with its worm-like appearance. Photo by Mella Panzella.

North American box turtles, genus *Terrapene*, are enormously popular in the herpetocultural hobby. Most keepers prefer them over the more demanding aquatic species. Photo of a neonatal Gulf Coast Box Turtle, *Terrapene carolina major*, by Mella Panzella.

warmer parts of the year (they will sit in very shallow waterpools in order to cool down). They are omnivorous when young, gradually becoming more herbivorous in their late years.

Box turtles make good pets and can be allowed free run of a backyard, outdoor pen, or similar. They should be fed on a variety of invertebrates and vegetable matter and are especially fond of slugs, snails, earthworms, and soft fruits. Raw, lean meat sprinkled with some vitamin/mineral supplement can be given regularly. Beware that "greedy" specimens don't become too fat and then are no longer capable of closing up!

North American box turtles are best purchased when they're young. Many older specimens currently being sold are wild-caught and usually do not adapt well to captivity. Photo of a juvenile Three-toed Box Turtle, *Terrapene carolina triunguis*, by Aaron Norman.

Getting North American box turtles to breed in captivity isn't particularly difficult, but you do need to provide them with plenty of space. Keeping them in an outdoor enclosure, at least during mating season, is the best approach. Photo of two Desert Box Turtles, *Terrapene ornata luteola*, by K. H. Switak.

The Ornate Box Turtle, *Terrapene ornata ornata*, is often called a "prairie animal" because of its fondness for treeless plains and rolling grasslands. It seems to have a particular liking for low-shrub areas with loose sandy soils. Photo by R. D. Bartlett.

Some tropical land tortoises occasionally are available. South American members of the genus *Geochelone* (of the family Testudinidae) are sometimes imported and frequently bred in captivity.

The best known and probably the most suitable

Revoltingly, Ornate Box Turtles have a habit of digging through piles of cow dung in the hopes of uncovering beetles and other insects. On a more palatable note, they also eat a wide variety of floral matter, including berries, melons, and leaves. Photo by Aaron Norman.

tortoise for captivity is the **Red-footed Tortoise,** *Geochelone carbonaria,* which reaches an adult length of about 20 in/50 cm. The common name arises from the red scales on the forelegs of most specimens; some have yellow scales. They also have attractive red or yellow markings on the otherwise dark-colored carapace and sometimes on the head. Since they come from tropical parts of northern South America, Red-foots must be kept warm all year long. They are best kept in a humid vivarium rather than a tortoise table and should be provided with a shallow water bath. They should be fed a variety of greens and fruits plus some animal material and a regular vitamin/mineral supplement.

The Leopard Tortoise, *Geochelone pardalis*, has been popular with hobbyists for many years. Being native to Africa, it requires a well-heated enclosure, and its eggs have a remarkably long incubation period—up to 230 days in captivity (even longer in the wild). Photo by Maleta and Jerry G. Walls.

The Red-footed Tortoise, *Geochelone carbonaria*, is one of the handsomest and most popular members of the family Testudinidae. A native of South America, it requires a well-heated enclosure and a broad diet (it is omnivorous). The young in particular need a highly varied diet or else they develop rickets. Photo by Mella Panzella.

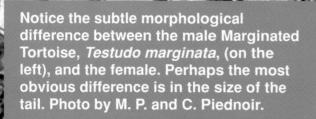

Notice the subtle morphological difference between the male Marginated Tortoise, *Testudo marginata*, (on the left), and the female. Perhaps the most obvious difference is in the size of the tail. Photo by M. P. and C. Piednoir.

The Yellow-footed Tortoise, *Geochelone denticulata*, occasionally is bred in captivity. Buying one, however, may be a lifetime commitment—specimens over fifty years old are not at all uncommon. Photo by Isabelle Francais.

The **Yellow-footed Tortoise**, *Geochelone denticulata*, is similar in size to the Red-foot (it grows a little longer—to 28 in/70 cm) and requires similar care. Another species, *G. chilensis*, is smaller, growing to around 9 in/22 cm, and is better suited to a tortoise table or dry vivarium. It also may be kept outdoors in warm, dry weather.

The **Indian Star Tortoise**, *Geochelone elegans*, is a popular species from, unsurprisingly, India. It makes a good pet but may be difficult to obtain. It reaches an overall length of 10 in/25 cm and has an attractive star pattern on its high-domed carapace. It should be kept in a heated indoor accommodation and fed on a diet of fruits and vegetables plus a little meat.

The **Leopard Tortoise**, *Geochelone pardalis*, comes from central and southern Africa and occasionally turns up in the pet trade. It grows to around 28 in/70 cm and has an attractive black and buff carapace said by some to resemble the spotting of a leopard. Its care is similar to that of the preceding species.

Leopard Tortoises, *Geochelone pardalis*, reportedly are becoming rarer in the wild, so anyone who has the opportunity to breed them should do so. Leopards are beautiful and gentle creatures that do well in captivity. Photo by K. H. Switak.

TT-013

TURTLES...AS A HOBBY, by W. P. Mara, 96 pages. Over 80 full-color photographs

YF-117

YOUR FIRST TURTLE, by Louis Dampier, 32 pages. Over 25 full-color photographs

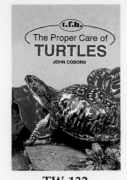

TW-132

PROPER CARE OF TURTLES, by John Coborn, 256 pages. Over 200 full-color photographs

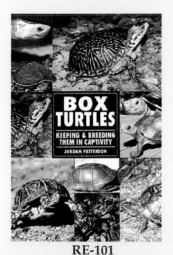

RE-101

BOX TURTLES, KEEPING AND BREEDING THEM IN CAPTIVITY, by Jordan Patterson. 64 pages. Over 60 full-color photos

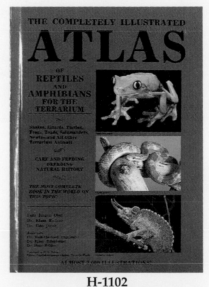

H-1102

THE COMPLETELY ILLUSTRATED ATLAS OF REPTILES AND AMPHIBIANS FOR THE TERRARIUM, by Fritz Jurgen Obst, Dr. Klaus Richter, and Dr. Udo Jacob. Edited in English by Jerry G. Walls. Over 800 pages. Over 1000 photographs and illustrations

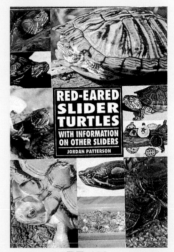

RE-109

RED-EARED SLIDER TURTLES, WITH INFORMATION ON OTHER SLIDERS, by Jordan Patterson. 64 pages. Over 60 full-color photographs

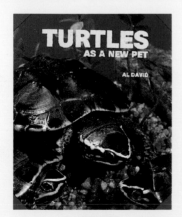

PS-307

TURTLES AS A NEW PET, by Al David. 64 Pages. Fully illustrated with color photos

TU-013

TURTLES FOR HOME AND GARDEN, by Willy Jocher. 128 pages. Fully illustrated with both color and black-and-white photos

KW-051

TURTLES, by Mervin F. Roberts. 96 pages

These and many other fine reptile and amphibian titles are currently being produced by T.F.H. Publications. Also worth checking out is T.F.H.'s new magazine, *Reptile Hobbyist*. Check with your local pet shop for details.

INDEX
Page numbers in **boldface** refer to illustrations.